Become an Impressive Leader in 5 Simple Steps

Successful, Influencer and Inspiring person

Table of Contents

Introductions

Chapter 1: What is an Impressive Leader?

Chapter 2: Mistakes Leaders Make and How to Fix Them

Chapter 3: Step 1 of becoming an Impressive Leader

Chapter 4: Step 2 of becoming an Impressive Leader

Chapter 5: Step 3 of becoming an Impressive Leader

Chapter 6: Step 4 of becoming an Impressive Leader

Chapter 7: Step 5 of becoming an Impressive Leader

Introductions

First off I want to thank you for taking time out your day to read *Become an Impressive Leader in 5 Simple Steps*. This book was made to help everyone because everyone has to be a leader at some point in life. Whether you're a parent, older brother/sister, business owner, or even a coach. Overall this book was to inform people and to help from my mistakes and my experience being a business owner myself and become a successful leader. I hope you enjoy the book, I put a lot of thought into it

Happy Reading!

Chapter 1: What is an Impressive Leader?

An impressive leader can be anything and people have their own opinion and definition. This is my definition of an impressive leader "An impressive leader is someone who creates an inspiring vision of the future for the team and does everything and anything they can to reach their goals and motivate others". It's not a perfect definition, but it sums everything up. Here is what the experts say:

Leaders are people who do the right thing; managers are people who do things right.

– Professor Warren G. Bennis

Leadership is the art of getting someone else to do something you want done because he wants to do it.

– Dwight D. Eisenhower

Being a leader isn't easy at all. Leaders have constant pressure on them and they have to be great at problem solving. In today's world on how fast things are changing, leaders are more worried than ever, it is hard to clarify around overall directing and while everything keeps changing it gets more difficult to find ways to support key resources and team in their pursuit of strategy. The leader always has a destination in mind. Thomas Edison did not start his projects to build a better candle, he wanted to find a whole new way to come up with something that seemed so impossible. To create something that no one could have thought of.

Having just a vision is all fancy, but it's not enough. Things need to be done or fixed and the only way to accomplish it is to take matters into your own hands and get it taken care of. There are so many core roles a leader must do like teaching, motivating, decision making, communicating, and constantly learning. Becoming a leader takes time, it doesn't happen overnight. I know you've heard of that about a thousand times, but it's really true.

Ask all of the greatest leaders that ever lived like Abraham Lincoln, Mahatma Gandhi, Nelson Mandela, Martin Luther King Jr, and even Adolph Hitler YES Adolph Hitler was a good leader ! But don't get me wrong I do not agree with his practices and his doings. I just want you to understand that the best leaders are old, it took time, hard work, and executions for them to become the legends they are now. Leaders also make mistakes. Don't beat yourself up because you make mistakes, we are all human and things get tough. You can sit down and study the real estate market all you want. It doesn't mean that your investment decisions are going to work every time. We wake up every day and take risk and not even know it. Just be a positive person and be good with people. It will take you a long way of not just being an impressive leader but a great person too.

Steve Jobs was kicked out of his own company. When Steve Jobs returned to Apple and turned the company into a sensational powerhouse, he was hailed as a genius and he pocketed billions. But that level of success had eluded Jobs for decades. After starting Apple with partner Steve Wozniak, Jobs was booted out of the company after too many failed projects. Resentful but determined, Jobs started a new company, next , whose hardware failed catastrophically. Fortunately, the software division was successful, and Apple's acquisition of that division put Jobs back in charge. The rest is history.

      Steve Jobs is lasting evidence that you should never count somebody out (even yourself). Instead of wallowing in self-defeat, he poured his efforts into new enterprises and constantly refined his visions until he earned his way back to the top of Apple. Even if someone pushes you back, you have to keep moving forward.http://www.inc.com/jayson-demers/7-challenges-courageous-leaders-overcome.html

Chapter 2: Mistakes Leaders Make and How to fix them?

There is no such thing as a "Perfect Leader". There is always a lesson to be educated and upgrades to be made. Here are some mistakes leaders make that you may not know were mistakes in the first place.

- **Giving your feelings access to the basic leadership process.**

In your own life, it's anything but difficult to give your sentiments around a circumstance a chance to impact the choice you make about it. In business, utilizing feelings as your sole avocation for anything is a terrible practice; your group needs to see the realities of having your back and your decisions in the event that you need them to trust you.

"When you're making decisions based on emotion ... the team may not truly understand the rationale behind the decision being made, and in many cases, rationale may not exist. This can lead to confusion, uncertainty of future roadmap plans or the validity of the decisions over time, slowly chiseling away at the effectiveness of the leader. Take a deep breath, step back and hold your tongue. Then think." – Christopher Ayala, CEO of Vertisense

- **Keeping away from problems**

A standout amongst the most troublesome leader needs to figure out how to handle contradictions or issues that emerge inside the gathering. You might be worried about the possibility that calling somebody in your group out for poor conduct or execution will make him or her not like you, however, over the long haul, it will hurt your entire staff progressively on the off chance that you don't stop an issue from developing in any way.

"Managers often veer away from confrontation and try to avoid it at all costs. But when performance or personality issues go unaddressed, they fester and set an overall tone that minimizes the urgency of correcting mistakes. If there is an issue, it's best to address it right away when the situation is fresh. Managers incorrectly assume that a problem is the result of incompetence or poor performance when in actuality it's often a result of of a misunderstanding of expectations. Create an environment that encourages continuous feedback and be exact with dates and expected outcomes." – Mark Feldman, vice president of marketing at Seven Step RPO

- **Putting up with the group's slack.**

Leaders are ordinarily contracted or elevated to their positions since they realize what should be done and how to do it. This might be joined by the mindset of, "On the off chance that you need something done well, do it without anyone else's help," which can be a perilous demeanor to have while dealing with a group. Finishing or tweaking your representatives' works since it's not to your enjoying, neglecting to delegate assignments makes more work for you, as well as keeps your group from achieving its maximum capacity.

- **Approving choices without a full understanding.**

As a leader, you will probably end up in a position to settle on decisions about things that are outside your territory of aptitude. For example, you may need to approve advertising methodologies or deals choices, despite the fact that your experience is in tech. Try not to settle on an official choice without counseling your employees in your organization who don't have the correct expertise in these situations.

- **Neglecting to recognize your group accomplishments.**

When you're made up for lost time in gatherings, telephone calls, and other everyday errands, you may not generally take an ideal opportunity to express your thankfulness for your group's diligent work. Workers wouldn't fret peruses in the event that you think they benefited an occupation, ensure you let them know, in a way that will impact them.

- **Not listening to yourself.**

You would prefer not to be the leader who steamrolls everybody and declines to consider the gathering's conclusions. In any case, you additionally would prefer not to twist around in reverse making others cheerful if their desires aren't what you accept is best for the business. Your supposition matters, as well, so you shouldn't be reluctant to comply with your gut nature when you know your right.

- **Lacking lowliness.**

At last, and maybe, in particular, leaders ought to never imagine that they're trustworthy. Your representatives need to realize that you're not above conceding your deficiencies, so show others how it's done and be straightforward with your group on the off chance that you accomplish something incorrectly or settle on a terrible choice.

Chapter 3: Step 1 of becoming an impressive Leader

- **Staying Humble**

A modest leader isn't pompous and knows about where he isn't the best. Part of being a leader is urging people around you to get included, give understanding that may miss, and help the organization or association develop to improve things. By monitoring your deficiencies, you can discover ranges for self-improvement and will have the capacity to delegate obligation and power to others that exceed expectations where you don't. You'll assuage yourself of anxiety in the fleeting and will improve as a leader and individual in the long haul. Part of being unassuming is perceiving where you can learn and enhance and after that imparting that information to others. Stories of deterrents and how you defeated them with the gathering around you are advantageous for the unit all in all. Every sees their worth being perceived and sees that despite the fact that you are in a higher position, regardless you have space to learn, pretty much as they do.

Humble leaders comprehend and apply a parity of being solid, yet tender. Leaders are always being tested by obstructions and workers, and a modest leader knows when the time has come to be firm in a heading or meeting and when he/she should be gentler. The same goes for adjusting individual achievement and the accomplishment of others. Offer the spotlight with others and perceive the individuals who have done well in the obligations they've been given. By finding the harmony amongst delicate and solid, you'll have the capacity to hold the admiration of people around you while as yet being an outlet for open discussion and comprehension. By demonstrating an ability to share the spotlight, others in your gathering will feel esteemed and value the acknowledgment.

Certainty is vital to excelling in life. It helps you improve at work, seeing someone, and in meetings. Being cocky can make you appear like a bastard. We as a whole realize that one individual that supposes they are the most grounded, sharpest, and only all-around best at everything. Honestly, we as a whole don't like that individual to some degree.

- **Staying Motivated**

Inspiration originates from consistent learning on the best way to be better. In this way, you ought to dependably be asking yourself, "What am I attempting to accomplish?" and "What do I have to figure out how to achieve my objective?" Understand this isn't about taking a workshop or perusing a book. It's about testing yourself to tackle something new and to extend yourself into another level of results.

The truth of the matter is that when you work on learning as a component of individual authority, you stay motivated, and you show signs of improvement results for yourself and for your work. By learning, you enable yourself to have, do and be whatever you pick. What's more, with strengthening comes certainty. You don't second-figure yourself or stress you'll fall flat since you know whether you fail to understand the situation, you'll have the capacity to make sense of how to hit the nail on the head.

Search for individuals whose style you like individuals who rouse you by the way they lead and the outcomes they get. Search out individuals who impact you and who appear to reflect parts of yourself. Associate with them to see what's feasible for you as a leader. Figure out how you can turn out to be more with the assistance of other people who have officially done what you need to do.

While keeping up a work/life equalization is not an approach to stay persuaded, it is an approach to keep from getting to be demotivated. When you're serving other people, you need to recollect to fill your own tank. Keep in mind that being a compelling and spurred leader ought to not come to the detriment of personal satisfaction, and personal satisfaction ought not to come to the detriment of business results. Work and life ought to have the capacity to exist together, joyfully and effectively. They can, and they have. The key is to characterize what that equalization looks like for you.

Staying persuaded in today's economy and work reality can be troublesome for anybody. In any case, when you assume liability for persuading yourself as well as other people, you turn into a genuine motivation and can better achieve your objectives. Subsequently, your vision, your potential, and your endeavors all leave an imprint. Yes, as you advance, there will be times you'll lose heart. You'll get occupied, you'll get drained, you'll overlook, you'll have mishaps, and you'll float away. Be that as it may, you won't get lost. You'll have a strong establishment for your proceeded with achievement, now and later on.

Chapter 4: Step 2 of becoming an impressive Leader

- A Leader is always the bigger person

More than we'd like we are confronted with circumstances where somebody may have exploited us. These sorts of circumstances can happen between companions, relatives, partners, or outsiders. When we get the short end of the stick or the terrible end of the deal or we are abused it is anything but difficult to need to counter. We need to "be the greater individual."

It's astonishing to me how these sorts of circumstances happen with individuals you think ought to know not. Be that as it may, these are the very circumstances we can get "made up for lost time in the web of" in the event that we aren't watchful. The best approach to release them is to be the greater individual and choose not to retaliate.

(The Bible says that when we bless someone who curses us we 'heap burning coals upon their head', meaning- there's no way to escape conviction. (Proverbs 25:21&22)

Life is too short to cling to things that take our bliss. Be the greater individual and let it go.

- Setting an example as a leader

Your state of mind matters more than everybody else's. As a leader, they are looking to you, looking for intimations and displaying your disposition. Keep in mind that somebody must infuse the inspirational state of mind, must grin to begin with, and must make it alright to consider issues proactively. On the off chance that you don't do it, who else will? Not your team…

Each leader needs those they prompt be learning, creating and developing. It is difficult to persuade them to do as such on the off chance that they don't see you doing it. On the off chance that you need others to be learners, you should be one first. In addition, the part of leader is sufficiently perplexing that there is continually something you can learn; continually something you can improve at.

The desires you have for others will affect their execution, decidedly or contrarily. Is it accurate to say that you are going first by raising your desire of others so they can assemble certainty, direness, and order to achieve those desires? It won't happen consequently. Set your desires of others, let individuals know you have confidence in them

If you want to affect and implement change you must be a champion of it. If you want the change to be successful, you must lead people towards it. This goes beyond corporate initiatives and major projects.

If you need to fabricate more trust in your association or with particular people, you should go first. Offer them trust. Be more reliable. Sitting tight for others to lead the pack, could be a long hold up. Broaden and offer trust first. Once in a while, you will get hurt, all the more regularly more prominent trust will construct.

On the off chance that you need the contribution of others, quit talking and begin inquiring. Make inquiries first. Make inquiries frequently. Great inquiries advance learning, data clarity and trade and engagement. In the event that you need these things, quit talking and begin inquiring.

Chapter 5: Step 3 of becoming an impressive Leader

Difference between a Leader and a Manager

You're most likely checking esteem, not including it, in case you're overseeing individuals. Just directors tally esteem; some even lessen esteem by handicapping the individuals who include esteem. In the event that a precious stone cutter is requested that report like clockwork what number of stones he has cut, by diverting him, his manager is subtracting esteem.

By complexity, leaders concentrates on making esteem, saying: "I'd like you to handle A while I manage." He or she produces esteem well beyond that which the group makes, and is as much a quality maker as his or her adherents seem to be. Showing others how it's done and driving by empowering individuals are the signs of activity based leadership.

Generally, as chiefs have subordinates and leaders have supporters, directors make circles of force while leaders make circles of impact. The snappiest approach to make sense of which of the two you're doing is to tally the quantity of individuals outside your reporting chain of command who come to you for advice. The more that do, the more probable it is that you are seen to be a leader.

- How to have Vision and Why it's Important to have one

- Consider one test inside your specialty, division or association.

- **Envision the 10,000 foot view.** Imagine the fantastic future achievement that you will acknowledge from the as good as ever circumstance, and the advantages to the association and to the representatives. This is your opportunity to be a genuine visionary. No fantasy is too enormous or excessively awesome. This is the "la-la-land" result you are seeing.

- Decide how you will convey your vision. What words and expressions will you utilize? In what environment will you convey your vision – in a workforce conference, one on one, with administrators and chiefs? In what manner will you convey the advantages to the staff and to the association? Record your thoughts on paper.

- Work on conveying what you have composed. Ensure it sounds earnest. Hone boisterously to yourself and to others. On the off chance that you don't trust it, nobody else will trust it either.

Vision can be characterized as a photo in the leader's creative ability that persuades individuals to activity when imparted compellingly, enthusiastically and plainly.

To be a visionary, a leader need have just an unmistakable vision without bounds. The troublesome undertaking is discussing that vision with clarity and enthusiasm keeping in mind the end goal to persuade and motivate individuals to make a move. A visionary leader who unmistakably and enthusiastically conveys his or her vision can inspire representatives to act with energy and reason, in this way guaranteeing everybody is progressing in the direction of a shared objective. The finished result is that everybody adds to the association's forward energy.

When you are prepared to convey your vision to your representatives, give them just the vision of accomplishment. Incredible leaders use vision as a device to move and rouse, not to direct. Try not to give your workers the progressions for accomplishing the vision, yet let them decide the techniques and strategies for accomplishing the objective. Incredible leaders know how to give the endowment of vision and after that progression away.

Chapter 6: Step 4 of becoming an impressive Leader

- Communicate with your team

To beat challenges in leadership is to energize open correspondence among colleagues. You are unfortunately mixed up in the event that you feel that your occupation as a group supervisor is to sit and rest. A leader needs to recognize what his colleagues are up to, however, yes there is a distinction amongst knowing and meddling.

You have to give your colleagues the space they require. The most ideal approach to win the trust of your colleagues is to sit with them once in consistently and enquire whether they are happy with their present part or not? Keep in mind, workers who are not fulfilled by their employments are the ones who make issues and sass their association. Give them a chance to explain their grievances and it is your obligation to give the most suitable arrangement at the earliest opportunity. Trust me, if minor issues are tended to at the soonest, you could never have an issue later on. Impart within the sight of all. Basic strategies should be talked about within the sight of all, so data comes to in its wanted structure.

- Richard Branson

Branson, likewise on the short rundown of wealthiest individuals on the planet, is as yet making waves as a trend-setter with different new undertakings reaching out from his center Virgin Records business. Be that as it may, if test scores and grades were a more genuine marker of future achievement, Branson never would have possessed the capacity to perform such enormity. Branson was, and is, dyslexic, a learning handicap in any event incompletely in charge of his awful state sanctioned test scores and beneath normal evaluations. In spite of those adolescence mishaps, Branson battled for his own thoughts and is at present regulating one of the greatest organizations on the planet.

Branson is an immaculate case of how constraints ought to never keep you down. Whether those impediments exist in your physical abilities, asset access, or elsewhere, there is basically no deterrent that can't be overcome. History is brimming with leaders who conquered target constraints to change the world.

- Great leaders are patient, How to stay patient?

It's generally simple to rapidly judge and impart your insight about how others deal with specific circumstances. As a leader, you should be target enough to venture back and expel yourself from individual conclusions and start to see the current circumstance through the other individual's Keep in mind that individuals running on vacant are inclined to become eager and lose their cool. Be sufficiently solid to handle the weight and sufficiently astute to be responsible and resolve the issue.

See the master plan and help your representatives draw an obvious conclusion toward an inevitable arrangement and assemble self-trust along the way.

Patience requires a leader to deliberately assess pressure focuses. How they are overseen by others may uncover critical thinking designs that can help us suspect the startling and inspire nearer to comprehension the underlying drivers of issues. However, that is not a viable alternative for being caring with your representatives and demonstrating that you think about their specific regions of concern and the strain focuses made.

Stay impartial and don't pick sides. As a leader, you should be greatly liberal and patient underweight with a specific end goal to consider it to be an open door beforehand inconspicuous. For instance, I as of late got to be disappointed with a worker that couldn't see what I was seeing for a specific customer. While my patience was being tried, it opened my eyes to comprehend the special ways this representative drew closer issues and helped me to better value her aims and key point of view.

Rehearsing patience obliges you to be an incredible audience and make inquiries. It requests that you take a full breath and let go of your own impatience to take care of an issue. Try not to be in a rush. Regard and grasp the procedure.

The force of a **grin** and an inspirational state of mind can amazingly affect the act of patience.

Effective leaders make **inquiries and look for direction constantly.** All things considered, they seem to know it all yet within, they have a profound hunger for information and continually are vigilant to learn new things in light of their dedication to improving themselves through the knowledge of others.

Numerous representatives in the work environment will let you know that their leaders have quit being instructors. Fruitful leaders never quit showing since they are so self-roused to learn themselves. They utilize educating to keep their associates very much educated and learned through insights, patterns, and other newsworthy things.

Fruitful leaders take an ideal opportunity to tutor their associates and make the venture to support the individuals who have demonstrated they are capable and anxious to progress.

Chapter 7: Step 5 of becoming an impressive Leader

- **Things leaders do every single day**

Many times leaders intimidate their colleagues with their title and power once they walk into an area. Fortunate leaders deflect attention off from themselves and encourage others to voice their opinions. They're specialists at creating others feel safe to speak-up and with confidence share their views and points of read.

Fruitful leaders are master chefs. They either encourage the exchange to enable their associates to achieve a key conclusion or they do it without anyone's help. They concentrate on "getting things going" at all times basic leadership exercises that support progress.

The best leaders comprehend their partners' mentalities, capacities, and ranges for development. They utilize this learning/understanding to challenge their groups to think and extend them to go after additional. These sorts of leaders exceed expectations in keeping their kin on their toes, never permitting them to get settled and empowering them with the devices to develop.

Effective leaders permit their associates to oversee them. This doesn't mean they are permitting others to control them but instead getting to be responsible to guarantee they are being proactive to their partner's needs.

Past simply tutoring and supporting chose representatives, being responsible to others is an indication that your leader is engaged more on your prosperity than simply their own.

Representatives need their leaders to realize that they are paying consideration on them, and they welcome any experiences along the way. Fruitful leaders dependably give criticism, and they invite corresponding input by making reliable associations with their partners. They comprehend the force of point of view and have taken in the significance of input at an opportune time in their vocation as it has served them to empower working environment headway.

Fruitful leader's adoration being leaders not for force but rather for the significant and deliberate effect they can make. When you have achieved a senior level of leadership, it's about your capacity to serve others, and this can't be refined unless you really appreciate what you do.

At last, effective leaders can maintain their prosperity by taking action and having an enjoyable time doing it.

Oprah Winfrey overcame a tragic past. After experiencing years of abuse from family members and friends, Winfrey ran away from home and bore a child at age 14 who died shortly after birth. Despite a childhood and early adolescence riddled with tragedy and adversity, Winfrey became an honors student in high school and earned a full college scholarship.

Today, she's instantly recognizable as one of the most successful television personalities and entrepreneurs in the world, with a net worth in the billions. http://www.inc.com/jayson-demers/7-challenges-courageous-leaders-overcome.html

Conclusion

- **Excuses**

The reason comes from the customary meaning of leadership. It likens leadership with a position and with power. On the off chance that we characterize leadership in an alternate way, it opens up an altogether new viewpoint for understudies. Imagine a scenario in which leadership was more about individuals seeking after a "calling" in life; a calling with which we will impact others in its satisfaction. Imagine a scenario where it had more to do with finding a zone of quality and in utilizing that quality, we'll actually impact others emphatically. We have picked this idea to characterize leadership. We trust it is basically utilizing our impact for a beneficial purpose.

We likewise trust impact and power are not one in the same. Your director can give you a position and with it comes power. That position empowers you to compel individuals to do what you need them to do. This is not leadership. It is burden. It might even be control or terrorizing, however, it isn't sound leadership. We trust your title can give you power, however, it can't give you impact. Solid impact is earned by the believably you convey to a relationship or association.

Normally, a few people are going to end up being preferred leaders over others. Some will really get to be phenomenal at arranging extensive groups of individuals, or at addressing expansive gatherings of individuals and throwing vision to them. Be that as it may, leadership isn't restricted to these abilities. On the off chance that it's just for the talented individuals, then we'll never fulfill the great that requirements to happen in our lifetime. It would resemble saying that nobody needs to serve who doesn't have the endowment of administration; or that you don't need to pay charges on the off chance that you don't have parcel of cash. That is ridiculous. We as a whole have the obligation to do what we can base on our qualities.

The best leaders don't simply move past an impediment, they discover significance in it, and use it further bolstering their good fortune. When you confront a test, you can't simply take a gander at how it's restricting you; you need to take a gander at how it transforms you, and how it could improve you.

How about we figure out how to lead and impact in a way proper with our skill, and not pardon ourselves. Leadership is an approaching each one of us, to some degree. It's about turning into the individual we were intended to be. It is less about position and more about manner. It is not such a great amount about prevalence but rather about administration in the range of our qualities. It has less to do with an arrangement of practices and more to do with a viewpoint with which we see life.

All leaders, in the end, face hardship. Extraordinary leaders beat those hardships and enhance themselves all the while. Whether you're a supervisor, a business person, a researcher, or a tutor, you need to take a gander at your weakest minutes as circumstances as opposed to confinements. Each deterrent, and each disappointment is simply one more stride toward your definitive destination, **Achievement.**

www.ingramcontent.com/pod-product-compliance
Lightning Source LLC
Chambersburg PA
CBHW070430190526
45169CB00003B/1485